When practicing yoga, it is important
to listen to your body and do only
what's comfortable for you.
Move mindfully. Be relaxed.
Never push yourself or force a pose.

When I Feel

Easy Yoga for Big Feelings

Kathy Beliveau

PHOTOGRAPHED BY
Jesse Holland

ILLUSTRATED BY
Julie McLaughlin

ORCA BOOK PUBLISHERS

Sometimes I feel happy.
Sometimes I feel sad.
But I have ways that help me
with feelings that I've had.

Sometimes I feel worried,
so I become a bee.
I hum and hum and buzz until
the worry's out of me.

When I feel anxious,
I tuck into my shell,
pretending I'm a tortoise,
silent, safe and well.

And if I'm feeling jumpy,
I act like I'm a frog!
I hop and leap and jump and then
I stretch out like a dog.

When I feel scattered,
I stand and lift one knee.
Then carefully I balance,
pretending I'm a tree.

And when I feel frightened,
I do the "scaredy-cat."
I arch my back and hisssss,
then curl up on my mat.

Sometimes I feel angry,
so I become the sea.
I breathe in deep an ocean breath
and breathe out peacefully.

If I am feeling silly,
I wiggle on the floor.
And when I need to feel brave,
I take a breath and roar!

At times I feel tired,
when everything is loud.
I close my eyes and make believe
I'm floating on a cloud.

I have so many feelings,
so many ways to be.
No matter what, they're all okay
because they're part of me.

Yoga Poses and Benefits

We all have feelings. And we have many different kinds of feelings. Our feelings are like messengers inside us. Practices like mindfulness and yoga help us pay attention to these messages and manage our feelings, which is important to our health and happiness.

Yoga means union, or "to unite or bring together." Yoga unites body, breath and mind and helps us relax, think more clearly and feel more balanced. It is a powerful practice that was developed in India over five thousand years ago and has become popular around the world.

When I Feel: Easy Yoga for Big Feelings shows us ways to calm, focus and relax our bodies and minds using yoga.

 BEE BREATH—When you hum, you create a vibration that helps release tension. The long exhalation of the "hummm" stimulates the parasympathetic nervous system and creates a relaxation response in your body.

 TORTOISE POSE—Bending forward and tucking in your head helps you tune out the world around you. This pose has a calming effect and counters overstimulation and anxiety.

 **FROG POSE**—Hopping up and down is a fun way to release excessive energy. Try croaking or sticking out your tongue to catch flies!

 **DOWNWARD DOG POSE**—This stretch calms your mind and is great for your spine.

TREE POSE—When you practice balancing on one foot (with or without support), you encourage your brain to focus your attention on one thing only—not falling over!

CAT POSE—Arching your back releases tension in your spine, and exhaling with the long *hisssss* calms your sympathetic nervous system.

OCEAN BREATH—Taking a deep breath and making a long *haaaaa* sound as you exhale releases pent-up energy, anger and frustration and soothes and settles the mind.

HAPPY BABY POSE—Rolling on your back and being silly like a baby calms your nervous system. Giggling is good for everyone!

LION POSE—Taking a deep breath, opening your mouth wide and unleashing a powerful roar relieves tension and can help build confidence and self-esteem.

CLOUD POSE, OR SAVASANA—Lying silent and still gives the body and mind a chance to pause and reflect and brings a feeling of calm, clarity and balance.

KATHY BELIVEAU's passion for yoga and nature shines through in her writing, presentations and workshops. She has studied yoga for children and yoga safety, and she is a certified yoga instructor. She is the author of *The Yoga Game* picture book series (Simply Read) and co-author of the *Strong Nations Yoga Cards*. Kathy lives on Vancouver Island, close to nature and the sea.

JULIE MCLAUGHLIN is an award-winning illustrator of numerous children's books, including *Pride Puppy!*, *Little Cloud*, and *Why We Live Where We Live*, winner of the 2015 Norma Fleck Award for Canadian Children's Non-Fiction. Her work with various editorial, advertising and publishing clients can be seen around the world. Julie grew up on the Prairies and now resides on Vancouver Island.

JESSE HOLLAND is a professional photographer based in Victoria, British Columbia. Although Jesse has been photographing families, couples and weddings for over ten years, this is her first time photographing for a children's book.

For Santiago, Everett and Theo, with happy feelings and endless love.
—K.B.

Text copyright © Kathy Beliveau 2021
Illustrations copyright © Julie McLaughlin 2021
Photos copyright © Jesse Holland 2021

Published in Canada and the United States in 2021 by Orca Book Publishers.
orcabook.com

Library and Archives Canada Cataloguing in Publication
Title: When I feel : easy yoga for big feelings / Kathy Beliveau ; photographed by Jesse Holland; illustrated by Julie McLaughlin.
Names: Beliveau, Kathy, 1962– author. | Holland, Jesse, photographer. | McLaughlin, Julie, 1984– illustrator.
Identifiers: Canadiana (print) 2021009642X | Canadiana (ebook) 20210096462 |
ISBN 9781459825840 (hardcover) | ISBN 9781459815780 (PDF) | ISBN 9781459815797 (EPUB)
Subjects: LCSH: Hatha yoga for children. | LCSH: Emotions in children. | LCSH: Exercise for children.
Classification: LCC RJ133.7 .B45 2021 | DDC j613.7/046083—dc23

Library of Congress Control Number: 2020951478

Summary: This instructional photographic picture book teaches children some basic yoga poses to help them accept and mindfully manage their (sometimes overwhelming) emotions.

Orca Book Publishers is committed to reducing the consumption of nonrenewable resources in the making of our books. We make every effort to use materials that support a sustainable future.

Orca Book Publishers gratefully acknowledges the support for its publishing programs provided by the following agencies: the Government of Canada, the Canada Council for the Arts and the Province of British Columbia through the BC Arts Council and the Book Publishing Tax Credit.

Cover and interior artwork by Julie McLaughlin
Photos by Jesse Holland
Edited by Liz Kemp
Design by Julie McLaughlin and Rachel Page

Printed and bound in China.

24 23 22 21 • 1 2 3 4